THE SU GLOBAL THINKING

~~KNOWLEDGE~~

BY

KNOWLEDGE

MUNYARADZI MUNENGE

MISSING ACKNOWLEDGEMEN
& DEDICATION

KNOWLEDGE

Table of Contents

THE SUPPOSE GLOBAL THINKING

Dimensional thinking is something that is always taken and considered as something that is for a certain class of people or object to a certain environment. Creation was made to be one not certain category of objects, lives and factors, hence the word creation in singular form.

Whenever we think of a dimensional thinking, we are refereeing to a level of mind functionality that depicts an idea or mind from God through human capacity and ability.

We have several dimensions of thinking in the following terms which are; **Human thinking, Animal/Fauna thinking, Robotic**

thinking and Passive/Object thinking. These four dimensions are derivatives from the ultimate thinking of God and the three of them are laid on the foundation of the five God give senses in Humanity which is the simulation of God's mind.

All the four the dimensional thinking are supposed and hoped to be the thing which sinks together with the synergy of the mind of God and the globe. This is because God is the one who created all the four-dimensional thinking according to his own thought, desire and willingness.

With this ordinarily, and obvious common knowledge we believe the mind of every person portrays the image of his creator who is the founder and foundation of the globe and universe at large. This can be simplified in the sense that, what someone says or does is exactly what they think or purpose in their mind, Proverbs 23:7.

To the abundant f the heart, the mouth speaketh, to the abundant of the heart; the mind thinketh and to the abundant of the soul and man behaves.

In this context we are saying the chief architecture of everything is God himself and we are like him in every aspect of our ideas, meditation, thinking and reaction. What it implies is, when we think we should think positive, giving an idea it must be a positive idea, every good of you must be a mirror to the good character of God.

HUMAN MIND AND THINKING

The human thinking is believed to be the most super thinking dimension among all and more active and have the power to create, innovate, initiate and built other thinking under the sun.

When God created humanity, his mind was to create himself and he thought of Adam to represent him in his image and after his likeness. When God said let us create man in our image and after our likeness, he meant the whole mind and thinking, which the engine of humanity is.

God is the one who should guard the mind of humanity because even the enemy panteth to grab human mind because he knows it is the only mind that represents God on earth. The enemy knows if he snatches human mind he has the soul and spirit of man and he can rule world.

The good thing is that human mind cannot accommodate both dominance of the God and dominance of the enemy. When the human mind accommodates the human thinking it means it flashes out the dominance of God. Like what is said by the bible in the book of James that; a well cannot produce sweet water and bitter water at the same time

The thinking or capacity of training an animal to live with man was an idea of God. He created that software when he created animals in the Garden of Eden and Adam was made to live in harmony with several herds and flocks of animals without human and wild animal conflict.

In Adam, he impacted and inset that mind to domesticate a dog, cat, cock and everything that is known as a pet or domestic animals in today's word. To this extend even the bible testifies exemplary, when Jesus said John 10: 27: My sheep hear my voice, and I know them, and they follow me, 28: And I give unto them eternal life; and they shall never perish, neither shall any man pluck them out of my hand. This sense indicated by Jesus and it fulfilled the mind of God between Human thinking and Animal thinking.

This was God in human capacity. God is a good shepherded Psalms 23. He can take care of everyone and a simple example was that of the Eden when he had various flocks of animals in their names and species.

It is suppose to be that dimensional thinking that every man in our **houses and family set ups** we must take responsibility of looking after our families and take our responsibilities so as to be real good shepherds. A good shepherded knows where good pastures are. A good shepherd knows where the fresh fountains of sweet waters are. A good shepherd knows the value of his flock work hard to improve the value of his flock.

A good shepherd who has the thinking of God avoids bitter waters for his pastures. Bitter waters for the flock abort production to the flock. This means that no fruits will be produced from the flock and this will kill and destroy the interest of the shepherd to his flock because there will be no multiplication.

God gave man the mind and ability to think and the power of multiplication, that means if man is not replenishing in doing good in the kingdom of God and in life in general; there is no reason to nature that mind.

The mind which is idle will die and bears no fruit. In the Book of John Chapter 15: 1-4, [1] I am the true vine, and my Father is the husbandman. [2] Every branch in me that beareth not fruit he taketh away: and every branch that beareth fruit, he purgeth it, that it may bring forth more fruit. [3] Now ye are clean through the word which I have spoken unto you. [4] Abide in me, and I in you.

Human thinking has the power and ability to build and to destroy, so as to that of God when he created the earth, and when he decided to destroy Sodom and Gomorrah it was his capacity to do that. He is the foundation of human thinking, man must not be a vessel to betray the efforts of God's initiatives, thinking and creation.

In the Bible, Psalms 8:6, It speaks of men created a little lower that Angeles and other versions say a little lower than God which implies that according to this level of faith Human thinking is the mother of all. Men was given dominion to rule everything under the sun according to the book of Genesis.

ANIMAL/FAUNA THINKING

Every animal that has a life on earth, that lives beneath the shallow and deep waters and those who crow over the surface has a certain level of dimensional thinking according to the order of God. God put the software of thinking in animal differently from that of Humanity and Robots (Modern Technology).

In the bible, it was Adam who named all animal in their names and the name would give an animal a behaviour that means the naming of animal was derived from Human mind and authority. Animal or Fauna thinking is a move or reaction from Humanity and its thinking.

Animal thinking functions under the dominance, instruction and control of human thinking. It is the mind of man that determine how the animal should live and behave.

Difference between human thinking and Animal thinking

Human thinking has two strong characteristics in that; it is authoritative and instructive whilst the Animal/Fauna thinking is submissive and obedient for it to function well in the ecosystem. That is why if you find a domesticated animal, it is governed by submission and obedience and that which is in their wild, when it comes to a homestead it is governed by submission because when it is chased away it will go when it is told to come back it will come back.

In any way when it disregard these two principles of submission and obedience the result of it is death either by the barrel of a gun, an arrow and spear or the most cruelty of man which is the taste of poison or by suffering negligence.

A lion can roar like and it gives itself an identity, a man may try to roar like a lion but it won't give him an identity of a lion because he has so many duties to control other animals, domesticated and wild animals. When a lion roars, it will think like a lion and other animals will run away. How a person thinks him and identity and character.

A lion can't roar and start to behave like pangolin. Lions have their characteristics that define them. Whenever an animal wants to supersedes its aggression capacity begets reaction which is very unpredictable.

ROBOTIC THINKING

This level of dimensional thinking is believed to be the best intelligent according to man's wisdom of this world. This thinking is a programmed thinking that is stored in whatever object or any living and non living creature. It is one of the thinking that is regarded as a volatile thinking in religious circles.

In this day and time there is a quite a unique Robotic notion especially on several Religious movement and denominations when people are told to believe without any discernment of reason to spiritual facts. They believe what they have been told by the founder of the church than the TRUE FOUNDER who is God or a TRUE CHURCH which is Jesus Christ and God himself.

So man believers in any of the world's religions they are so much comfortable in what they have been programmed and to some extend it is good for better administration of function of the church or organisation.

The danger of Robotic thinking is that the Chief Architecture may decided to change the syntax of the program at any given time and as human or machine you may need to adjust and rethink which may cause loss of memory of thinking fatigue.

Robotic thinking is a fed process to regurgitate the necessary output that will benefit the society and it is based on what is needed on the ground. So many people are deceived by the things that they see on their day to day life and they put all their focus in that.

Most famous things do not mean anything out of it but it is good in a few people's eyes. So many people lost their good values and many life principles by being fed with information that do not help their life circumstances because they have Robotic mindset.

It is so hard for a person to have a paradigm shift when they have been fed for so many years with the same information, whether good or bad information.

Robotic information is generally not preferred way of thinking in the Christian world because sometimes a program may be bigger than the storage capacity of the person receiving it and it may cause crush.

Durability on storing the information is a very big disadvantage because information or doctrine may be stored today and a day after tomorrow the information is corrupt and disregarded.

Personally, I don't prefer preachers of the Gospel of Jesus Christ to preach to people with their good vocabulary and enticing words of man's wisdom, that will complicate the whole essence of the gospel. I prefer preacher to preach the goodness of God and good news of Jesus Christ, it is easy to store the goodness and good news of God than to store so many words from human's wisdom.

There are so many life incidents that can corrupt, interject the processing of Robotic information which are in most cases family, financial, economic and general social matters. The operation of a Robot is determined and influences by those aspects that surrounds it for it to manifest its functionality.

It is a risk in that when an event is influenced by what it is around the ecosystem, it means it lacks self driven values and rights in the kingdom of God. They do everything to please and impress the ecosystem where it abides.

PASSIVE/OBJECT THINKING

Passive thinking is also one of the thinking emanated from God's mind. This is the thinking that is enforced by divine thinking and Humanity for good example; all the non-living things they have reaction to a certain environment or any activity that happens under the sun.

Waters of the rivers can flow and water is known to flow towards gradient in science but in the mind of God it was his thinking and it is a principle that cannot be reversed.

The sun give light to the world and it is the thinking of God which gave the sun light to shiny upon the earth. His mind is functioning in the sun and the sun cannot speak its mind directly but it stores the mind and thinking of God i.e., Passive thinking.

It is true that thinking is the capacity of living and non-living organisms to react and give results; this is according to how I view live on earth.

In all this; what we are saying is, we may think, we may react, lest we forget that all what we call our mind, is centred on the mind of God. Theoretical thinking and practical thing, all is derived from the super mind of God.

Scientific inventions and innovations are a gift from the mind of God whether the person is a believer of not because God is not a respecter of man.

Printed in Great Britain
by Amazon

38356187R00015